M is for Majestic

A National Parks Alphabet

Written by David Domeniconi and Illustrated by Pam Carroll

Sleeping Bear Press
310 North Main Street, Suite 300
Chelsea, MI 48118
www.sleepingbearpress.com

Sleeping Bear Press is an imprint of The Gale Group, Inc.,
a division of Thomson Learning, Inc.

Printed and bound in Canada.

10 9 8 7 6 5 4 3 2 1

Library of Congress Cataloging-in-Publication Data
Domeniconi, David.
M is for majestic : a national parks alphabet / by David Domeniconi ;
illustrated by Pamela Carroll.
p. cm.
Summary: Examines the history and lore of America's national parks
from Acadia National Park to Zion National Park.
ISBN 1-58536-138-0
1. National parks and reserves-United States-Juvenile literature.
2. English language-Alphabet-Juvenile literature. [1. National parks
and reserves. 2. Alphabet.] I. Carroll, Pamela, ill. II. Title.
SB482.A4 D66 2003
333.78'3'0973—dc21   2003010467

To Janet, of course, and for the girls, Veronica and Victoria.
Special thanks to good friends Pam and Chris Carroll.
And thanks to all the folks in the national parks across the country
for answering my annoying e-mails. Apologies to Woody Guthrie.

DAVID

∞

To my precious sister Betty and visionary John Muir, two kindred spirits
who found in nature a timeless beauty forever fresh and new.

PAM

"Climb the mountains and get their good tidings. Nature's peace will flow into
you as sunshine flows into trees. The winds will blow their own freshness into
you, and the storms their energy, while cares will drop off like autumn leaves."

—*John Muir*
Our National Parks, *1901*

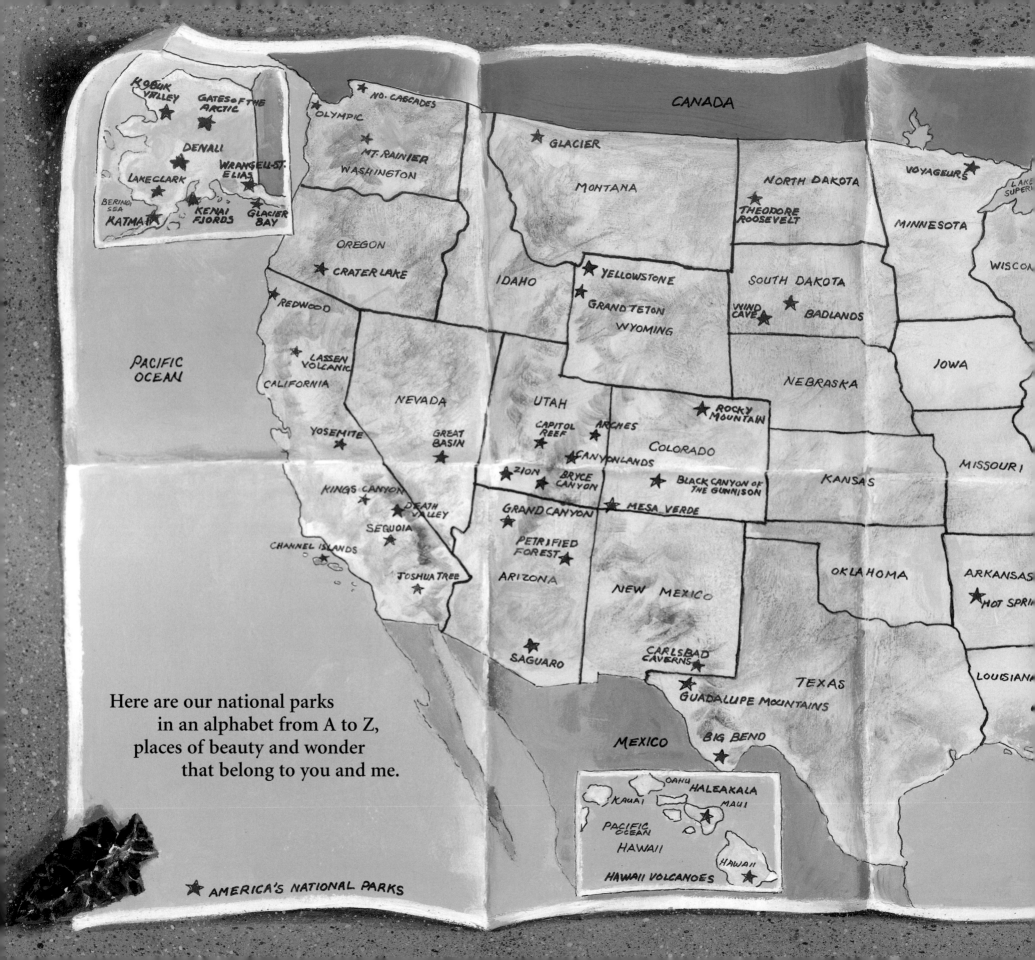

Here are our national parks
in an alphabet from A to Z,
places of beauty and wonder
that belong to you and me.

There is land, millions of acres of the world's most beautiful scenery—mighty mountains, wild rivers, fiery volcanoes, huge glaciers, vast forests, tropical islands—and it all belongs to you and me. In 1872, after learning about the great geysers of Yellowstone, Congress voted to create the world's first national park, a wilderness preserved just for the people of this country. It was such a good idea, other parks soon followed—Sequoia, Yosemite, Kings Canyon, and then the Grand Canyon and many more. Today, there are over 50 national parks, and new ones are being established every few years. Each park is created with the same idea—to preserve forever the natural wonders of this magnificent and majestic country.

In **Acadia National Park**, along the rugged coast of Maine, deep forests grow right down to the water's edge. Most of the park is on Mount Desert Island, an island with seaside villages and historic lighthouses. Acadia is unusual in that most of the parkland was donated by private individuals who wanted to preserve the natural beauty of the area. This is one of our smallest but one of our most visited national parks.

Get on a plane in Los Angeles and 14 hours later you'll be in **National Park of American Samoa**, a tropical paradise with sandy beaches, coral reefs, volcanic islands, and rain forests. Watch the skies at night for flying foxes, fruit bats with a wingspan of three feet.

A is for Acadia,
where the mountains meet the shore,
and the forest stands silent
beside the ocean's roar.

A

a

The world's greatest collection of natural stone arches can be found in the high desert of Utah at **Arches National Park**. More than 2,000 of these amazing sculptures have been carved out of the red rock through a combination of wind, water, and time.

B b

You wouldn't think anything could survive in **Big Bend National Park** in Texas, but this fiery desert is full of life. Lizards, snakes, scorpions, mule deer, rabbits, kangaroo rats, bats, javelinas, roadrunners, and many more desert creatures make their home in this dry land. Big Bend has more kinds of cacti and birds than any other U.S. national park. The southern edge of the park follows the winding path of the Rio Grande River, the border between the United States and Mexico.

In **Badlands National Park** in South Dakota, craggy hills rise in a wall across the prairie. Native Americans and pioneers found it almost impossible to travel across these hills and gave this place the name "badlands."

Roadrunner at Big Bend

Big Bend National Park, Texas

Gumbo lily from the Badlands

Badlands National Park, South Dakota

Golden Eagle

Spotted in Bryce Canyon

Thor's Hammer at Bryce Canyon National Park, Utah

B is for Big Bend,
a desert wonderland,
way down south in Texas
along the Rio Grande.

Black Bear

Seen at Black Canyon

Black Canyon of the Gunnison
National Park, Colorado

Manatees in the Florida waters at Biscayne
National Park

Sunflowers

from the
banks of
Gunnison River

Bryce Canyon National Park in Utah is famous for its incredible rock formations. Many of these odd shaped rocks look almost alive and have been given names like Queen Victoria, The Pope, The Poodle, and Thor's Hammer.

Black Canyon of the Gunnison National Park in Colorado preserves one of the steepest, deepest, and narrowest canyons in the U.S. At the bottom of the canyon, one of the last wild stretches of the Gunnison River runs between walls of sheer black rock.

If you want to get a good look at **Biscayne National Park** in Florida, you'll have to go underwater. There you'll find a brilliant world of coral reefs, brightly colored tropical fish, turtles, sharks, and rare manatees.

If you are looking for the deepest and the bluest lake in the United States, go to **Crater Lake National Park** in Oregon. Crater Lake was created 7,700 years ago when Mount Mazama exploded in a massive volcanic eruption. A six-mile-wide hole was left behind. Melting snow and rain filled the crater with water. Because it is so deep, 2,000 feet, and its water is so clear, Crater Lake has been called the world's bluest lake.

Cuyahoga Valley National Park in Ohio preserves the area around the historic Ohio and Erie Canal that opened in 1827. Between two large cities, this park is an oasis of open land along the Cuyahoga River, home to herons, bluebirds, and beavers.

C is for Crater Lake,
an unforgettable view
of water that's been called
the bluest of the blue.

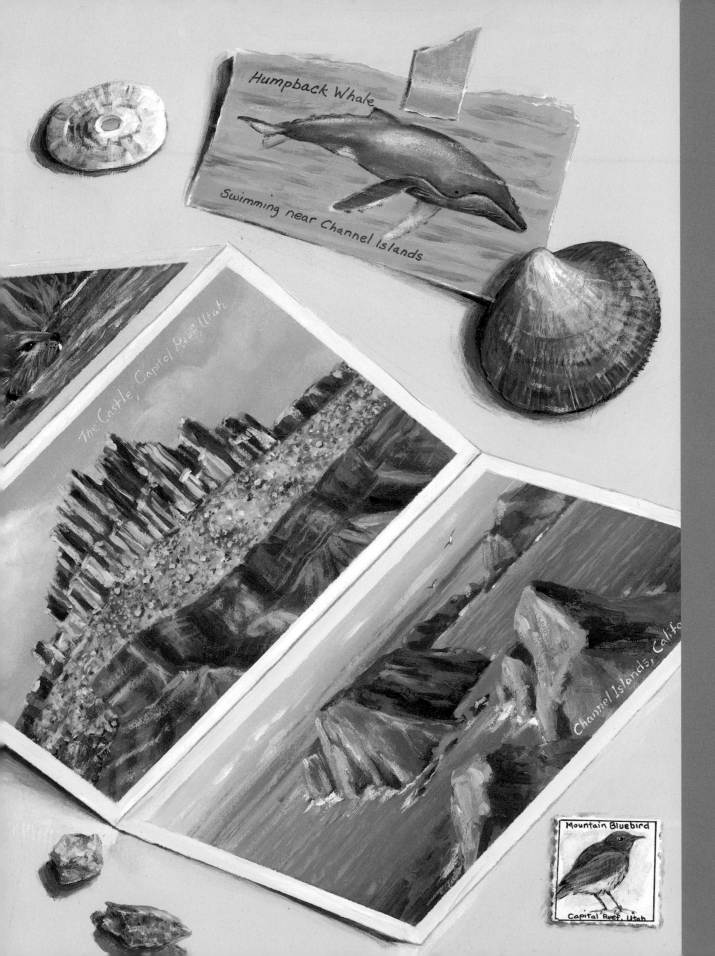

Humpback Whale

Swimming near Channel Islands

The Castle, Capitol Reef, Utah

Channel Islands, Califor

Mountain Bluebird

Capital Reef, Utah

In **Capitol Reef National Park**, a hundred-mile-long line of jagged hills, Waterpocket Fold rises up like a gigantic wrinkle in the Utah desert.

Channel Islands National Park, five islands off the coast of California, is the home of the giant elephant seal, five other kinds of seals, sea otters, and many sea birds. Gray whales pass by the park on their way from Alaska to Mexico and back again.

C c

Dry Tortugas National Park in Florida is actually quite wet. With the exception of a few low islands and Fort Jefferson, a military outpost unused since 1873, almost all of the park is underwater. There you'll find untouched coral reefs, sea turtles, and shipwrecks. These islands became known as the Dry Tortugas because they have no fresh water.

If you want to get really low, go to **Death Valley National Park** in the California desert. A dry lake called Badwater has the lowest elevation in the United States at 282 feet below sea level. Death Valley is also the hottest spot in the U.S. with a recorded temperature of 134 degrees Fahrenheit.

D is for Dry Tortugas
in the far-off Florida Keys.
Many a ship has found a home
at the bottom of its seas.

Mount McKinley, Denali National Park, Alaska

Racetrack, Death Valley California

D d

It's a bit of a climb to the top of **Denali National Park and Preserve** in Alaska. You'll have to hike 20,320 feet up to reach the summit of Mount McKinley, the tallest peak in North America. Denali ("The Great One") is the native Alaskan name for Mount McKinley.

The miles of saw grass in **Everglades National Park** in Florida is really a river—a river only six inches deep but fifty miles wide. This river is the lifeblood of the park's many creatures—hundreds of types of birds, turtles, panthers, manatees, and alligators. As the river flows to the sea, the saw grass turns into mangrove swamp—the home of the crocodile. Crocodiles are not as heavy as alligators, but they are faster and more dangerous. The sharp lower teeth sticking out of the crocodile's mouth give the croc its smile. In recent years, much of the park's water has been taken by cities and farms, making the Everglades our most threatened national park.

E is for Everglades,
miles and miles and miles
of saw grass and swamp
and smiling crocodiles.

Ff

$F$is for Kenai Fjords,
clear bays and icy peaks,
where birds fly underwater
flashing red and yellow beaks.

You won't need to bring your cooler to **Kenai Fjords National Park** in Alaska. Almost half of the park is covered with ice. The Harding Icefield alone is 300 square miles and nearly a mile thick. The Kenai Fjords are deep, narrow bays along the Gulf of Alaska. The shoreline here is packed with sea life—Stellar sea lions, sea otters, whales, and many sea birds. The horned puffin is a funny looking bird with a red and yellow beak. The puffin's short wings make it a clumsy flier, but once underwater the puffin glides gracefully through the sea.

Of all sights in our national parks, **Grand Canyon National Park** in Arizona just might be the grandest. The view from the South Rim draws visitors from around the world. Looking down, it is almost a mile to the bottom of the canyon and the Colorado River. The other side of the canyon, the North Rim, is only 10 miles away, but you'll have to make a five-hour drive around the canyon to get there. Scientists have many theories how this incredible place came to be, but no one is exactly sure how the Grand Canyon was created.

If you're looking for one place with a sagebrush desert, high mountains, a glacier, limestone caves, and some of the world's oldest trees—you'll have to go to **Great Basin National Park** in Nevada.

Gg

Ancient Bristlecone Pine at Great Basin National Park, Nevada

G is for Grand Canyon a place that has been found to be the world's most beautiful hole in the ground.

Ground squirrel at Great Basin

Grand Canyon National Park, Arizona

Guadalupe Mountains National Park in Texas

Texas Bluebonnet

Mountain Goats at Glacier National Park, Montana

Caribou at Gates of The Arctic National Park, Alaska

Forget-me-not from Alaska

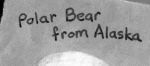

Polar Bear from Alaska

Glacier Bay National Park, Alaska

Tip of branch from Western Hemlock

The striking mountains rising out of the desert in **Guadalupe Mountains National Park** in Texas were once an underwater reef. Scientists from all over the world come to study the marine fossils in an area some believe to the most beautiful in all of Texas.

A million acres of some of our most beautiful mountain scenery, **Glacier National Park** in Montana is home to bald eagles, elk, wolves, mountain goats, bighorn sheep, and hundreds of grizzly bears.

It would be hard to find a wilderness wilder than **Gates of the Arctic National Park and Preserve** in Alaska, a park without roads or trails. Every year hundreds of thousands of caribou migrate across its frozen plains.

From a boat in **Glacier Bay National Park and Preserve** in Alaska, you can see and hear icebergs being made. Giant blocks of ice break off the glaciers at the water's edge and fall into the water with a crash that sounds like thunder.

H h

Hot Springs National Park, Arkansas

Haleakala National Park, Hawaii

Thanks to some of the world's most active volcanoes, **Hawaii Volcanoes National Park** is getting bigger every year. When Mauna Loa and Kilauea erupt, towers of red-hot lava shoot hundreds of feet in the air and rivers of molten rock run down the mountains. When the lava reaches the sea, steam rises in hissing clouds. Not long after the lava cools, plants sprout on the rocks and the big island of Hawaii gets bigger.

The giant volcano at **Haleakala National Park** on the Hawaiian island of Maui has been quiet for 200 years. These slopes are the home of the silversword, a plant found nowhere else in the world, and the rare Hawaiian goose, the nene.

Our smallest national park, **Hot Springs National Park** in Arkansas, protects the woods and historic bathhouses in an area famous for its pure and, some say, healing water.

H is for Hawaii Volcanoes
a restless park that grows,
    when fiery mountains erupt
    and red-hot lava flows.

Howling hasn't always been heard at **Isle Royale National Park** in Michigan. Only 50 years ago, timber wolves first made their way across frozen Lake Superior to Isle Royale. On the island, they found lakes and forests full of beaver and moose. The wolves stayed, and today the park is one of the few places in the lower 48 states where timber wolves run free.

I i

I is for Isle Royale,
  the island home of the moose,
    and a sight rarely seen,
      timber wolves on the loose.

J j

J is for Joshua Tree,
under a desert sky.
Yuccas stand and point the way
with branches held high.

You won't often see a plant as strangely beautiful as the yuccas of **Joshua Tree National Park** in California. Up to 40 feet tall and as old as 800 years, they grow in oddly twisted shapes on the Mojave Desert. In the 1800s, Mormons traveling through the desert named the yuccas after Joshua in the Bible. Like Joshua, the branches of the trees seemed to be pointing the way to the Promised Land.

If you want to take a stroll around General Sherman, the world's biggest tree, you'll have to visit **Sequoia and Kings Canyon National Parks** in California. Our second national park, Sequoia was established in 1890 to protect the world's largest trees, the giant Sequoias. Right next door, Kings Canyon National Park was created a short time later. The two parks have been run as one since 1945. There, you'll also get to see the 8,000 foot-deep Kings Canyon and Mount Whitney, the tallest mountain in the lower 48 states.

ALASKAN BROWN BEAR

Katmai Park

Sand Dunes at Kobuk Valley

K is for Kings Canyon,
 deeper than the Grand,
and right next door a tree
 that's the biggest in the land.

Katmai National Park and Preserve
in Alaska is famous for the Valley of Ten
Thousand Smokes, a valley covered in volcanic ash, and the Alaskan brown bear, the
world's largest land carnivore (meat eater).

In **Kobuk Valley National Park** you'll find
wild Alaskan mountains, forests, and rivers
and a whole lot of sand. Hundreds of
square miles of the park are covered with
barren sand dunes. Summer temperatures
here can reach 100 degrees Fahrenheit.

L¹

L is for Lake Clark
as lovely as a dream
with rivers running red,
when the salmon swim upstream.

The fishing is fine in **Lake Clark National Park and Preserve** in Alaska and not just for those with a rod and reel. Every June, when millions of sockeye salmon fill the rivers, Alaskan brown bears catch their limit. The salmon are making their way upstream against rapids and waterfalls to lay their eggs in the shallow streams around Lake Clark. At times, so many salmon fill the rivers the water looks red.

Lassen Volcanic National Park in California is a place of boiling mud, steam, and sulfur. Lassen Peak is quiet now but was the site of a mighty eruption in 1915.

When two cowboys discovered the cliff dwellings at **Mesa Verde National Park** in Colorado in 1888, these stone cities had already been empty for 700 years. Even the Navajo did not know who had lived in these intricate houses. The Navajo called the cliff dwellers the Anasazi, "the ancient ones." Cities like the Cliff Palace were built 800 years ago. But after only a hundred years, the cliff dwellings were abandoned. Years without any rain forced the ancient people to leave Mesa Verde. And where they went, no one can be sure.

m

M

M is for Mesa Verde,
    cities built long ago,
by an ancient people
    whose name we'll never know.

Mammoth Cave National Park in Kentucky is the site of the world's longest cave. So far, 350 miles of underground passages have been discovered. Many miles of the cave are still waiting to be explored.

It takes two days to climb to the top of **Mount Rainier National Park** in Washington State. Bring your ice axes and spiked shoes because you will have to cross jagged glaciers to reach the summit. This 14,000-foot mountain is actually a giant, sleeping volcano.

N n

In **North Cascades National Park** in Washington State, it's all about the glaciers. Three hundred frozen fields, half the glaciers in the lower 48 states, cover the park. All these rugged mountain peaks of ice and snow make for some rough hiking. But the more it snows, the better the snowshoe rabbit likes it. Snowshoe rabbits get their name from the thick, padded paws that allow them to walk on snow. Deep snow makes it easier for the snowshoe rabbit to get close to the tasty leaves on high branches.

N is for North Cascades
with glaciers wherever you go,
and rabbits wearing shoes
made specially for the snow.

If you plan to visit **Olympic National Park** in Washington State, bring along your galoshes. In a place called the Ho Rain Forest it rains 12 to 14 feet a year. That is a lot of rain. In this fairytale forest, tree branches are draped with hanging moss. Ferns and mushrooms and rotting tree trunks carpet the forest floor. Only a few spots of sunlight find their way down through the trees. This dim, green world is the home of elk, squirrels, tree frogs, and giant slugs.

O is for Olympic
where the rain takes no rest,
and moss and ferns grow wild
in an enchanted forest.

P is for Petrified Forest
    with many strange sights to see,
a desert that's been painted
        and rocks that once were trees.

P p

The desert in **Petrified Forest National Park** in Arizona hasn't really been painted. This land came to be known as the Painted Desert because of its brilliantly colored hills. And all the rocks here that look exactly like fallen logs really were once trees. Millions of years of soaking in mud and water and minerals turned the wood into stone. To protect these rare rocks the Petrified Forest was named our second national monument and later a national park.

If you ever get the urge to go spelunking (cave exploring), you'll want to visit **Carlsbad Caverns National Park** in New Mexico, one of the deepest and largest caves in the world. You can walk or take an elevator 700 feet down to a world of stalactites, stalagmites, and underground rooms with names like the Hall of Giants and Bottomless Pit. In the Queen's Chamber, rock walls appear to flow like lovely drapery. An equally amazing sight happens at sunset on summer evenings when a half-million Mexican free-tailed bats fly out of the caves to hunt for insects.

Q is for the Queen's Chamber,
but you won't find a crown,
in this room in Carlsbad Caverns
seventy stories down.

Redwood Park, California

The Great Divide, the highest range of mountains in North America, runs right through the middle of **Rocky Mountain National Park** in Colorado. Here you'll find 100 mountain peaks over 10,000 feet tall. These mountains are dotted with beautiful meadows and Alpine lakes. The symbol of the park, the Rocky Mountain bighorn sheep, covers all this high ground and can easily climb dangerously steep rock faces.

Some of the world's tallest trees live in **Redwood National Park** on the California coast. This park preserves one of the few untouched stands of these great trees.

R is for Rocky Mountain
    as high as it is steep,
        but it's just a walk in the park
            for the nimble bighorn sheep.

Rr

It would be hard to find a place with more varieties of plants and trees than **Great Smoky Mountains National Park** in North Carolina and Tennessee. The famous smoky haze over these mountains is created when the vapors given off by all this plant life mix with moist air from the Gulf of Mexico. This land was the original home of the Cherokee who were forced to leave in 1832 in what has become known as The Trail of Tears.

If you like big cactus, head to **Saguaro National Park** in Arizona. There you will see miles of the Sonoran desert filled with giant saguaro, cacti that can grow up to 50 feet tall.

Shenandoah National Park in Virginia is the home of the Blue Ridge Mountains, a range covered by lush hardwood forests and crisscrossed by many streams and waterfalls.

S is for Great Smoky Mountains
with a mist plain to see,
over a land once known as
the home of the Cherokee.

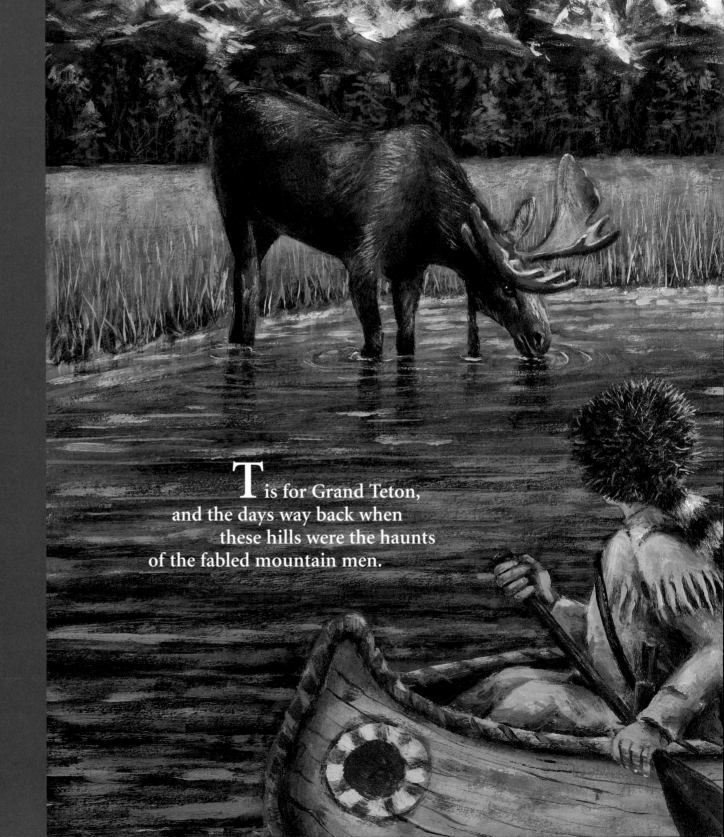

You can look but you probably won't find a more beautiful mountain scene than the Rocky Mountains in **Grand Teton National Park** in Wyoming. From a deep valley called Jackson Hole, the Tetons rise straight up in a jagged wall of granite. Back in the 1820s, this was the territory of the mountain men. These legendary trappers had names like Jedediah Smith and "Broken Hand" Fitzpatrick. Miles from any help, they wandered alone through the snow, hunting for beaver. Danger was on all sides—the cold, grizzly bears, and the trappers' sworn enemies, the Blackfeet. By the 1840s, most of the beaver were gone, and so were the mountain men.

T is for Grand Teton,
and the days way back when
these hills were the haunts
of the fabled mountain men.

Tt

U is for Upheaval Dome,
a most unusual sight,
a great big hole in Canyonlands
made by a meteorite.

Upheaval Dome, Canyonlands Utah

From a place called Island in the Sky, you can look out over **Canyonlands National Park** in Utah. There you will see an amazing desert landscape of deep river canyons, distant peaks that look like ruined castles, and a great big hole in the ground—Upheaval Dome. Scientists believe a giant meteorite slammed into the earth a few thousand years ago and made this three-mile-wide hole.

Canyonlands also contains some of the most unusual pictographs found in the Southwest. Pictographs are the ancient drawings carved into rock walls by early Americans thousands of years ago. Many of these drawings are of people and animals, but many of them are also of strange figures, creatures that look as if they came from another world.

V v

Down in the Caribbean, on the U.S. Virgin Island of St. John, you'll find **Virgin Islands National Park**, a park of green hills, blue water, and white sand beaches. Just off the beautiful beach at Trunk Bay is a nature trail made for snorkelers. Buoys lead the way along a coral reef that is home to parrot fish, turtles, eels, sea horses, and many other types of brilliantly colored fish and coral.

If you like canoeing and kayaking, **Voyageurs National Park** in Minnesota is the place. A land of lakes and bays full of loons and beavers, the park is named after the famous French-Canadian traders who paddled canoes loaded with furs and supplies across thousands of miles in these waters.

V is for Virgin Islands
where a nature trail begins
underneath the waves
so bring your mask and fins.

Wind Cave National Park in South Dakota was once a tourist attraction known as "the Great Freak of Nature." With over a hundred miles of narrow tunnels, this cave is one of the longest in the world. Wind Cave got its name from the gusty, whistling wind that blows in and out at the mouth of the cave. Aboveground in the park, you'll find one of the last open pieces of the Great Plains and many prairie dog towns. Not millions but billions of prairie dogs once lived on the grassland that stretched across the United States from Texas to Canada.

Mt. St. Elias, Wrangell-St. Elias National Park, Alaska

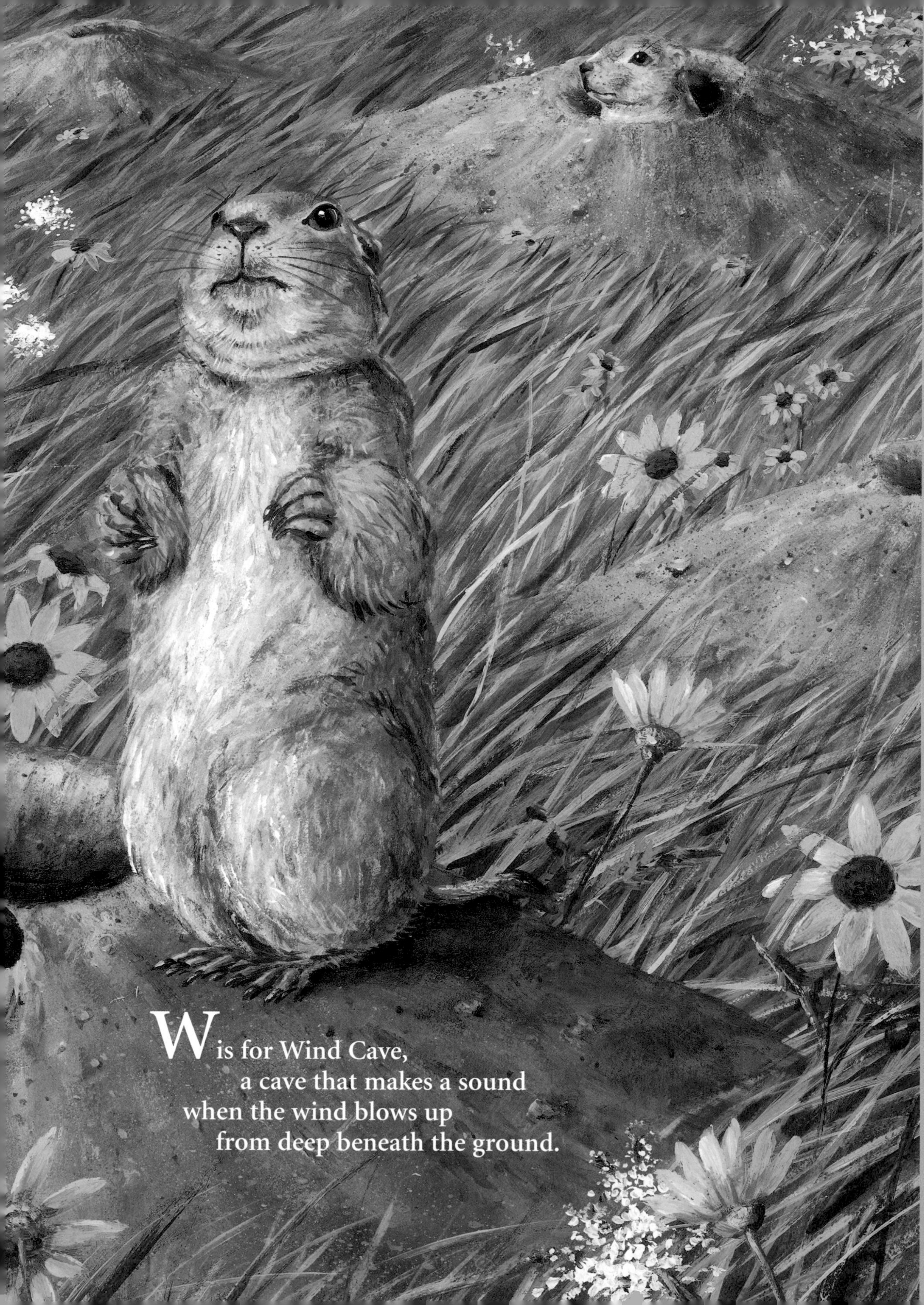

W is for Wind Cave,
a cave that makes a sound
when the wind blows up
from deep beneath the ground.

Wrangell-St. Elias National Park and Preserve in Alaska is our largest national park. Bigger than the country of Switzerland, the park is a rugged land of ice and snow and few roads. Many of the park's giant glaciers and mighty mountains are still waiting to be explored.

W
w

X is for the Long X Trail,
where you will get to know,
Theodore Roosevelt Park
and the last of the buffalo.

President Theodore Roosevelt

When settlers first saw the Great Plains, some 60 million buffalo roamed across this country. By 1883, when Teddy Roosevelt (our twenty-sixth president) came West, the bison had been hunted until only a few thousand remained. **Theodore Roosevelt National Park** in North Dakota preserves an area of the rugged Dakota Badlands where Roosevelt had a cattle ranch. In those days, cowboys drove great herds of longhorn cattle up from Texas to North Dakota along the park's Long X Trail, a trail named after the X brand of the Long X Ranch. Today, buffalo still roam the park, but only a few hundred remain.

X
X

Yy

Our first national park—**Yellowstone National Park** in Wyoming, Idaho, and Montana— was the world's first national park. In 1872, Congress created the park to protect the world's largest collection of geysers. Old Faithful, the most famous of the geysers, can shoot water 200 feet into the air. Geysers occur when water seeps down, comes into contact with the Earth's red-hot interior, and erupts to the surface. Old Faithful doesn't actually go off on the hour, but by using a simple formula park rangers can study the last eruption and predict the next eruption to within minutes. Yellowstone is a natural wonder—not only of geysers, but also of mountains, forests, rivers, waterfalls, and wildlife. Yellowstone has the largest herds of free-roaming elk and bison in the lower 48 states.

Y is for Yellowstone
and you can count the hour
    when Old Faithful blows its top
in a show of geyser power.

Greetings from Yosemite

There are valleys and then there is "The Valley" in **Yosemite National Park** in California, one of our national treasures. Cut by glaciers during the last ice age, Yosemite Valley is seven miles long, up to a mile wide, and almost a mile deep. Five of the world's 10 highest waterfalls drop off its walls of polished granite. El Capitan and Half Dome, two of Yosemite Valley's dramatic cliffs, are some of the most famous sights in our national parks.

There is only one way in and out of the Narrows, one of the remarkable canyons in **Zion National Park** in Utah. It is almost 2,000 feet from the bottom to the top of the canyon, but in some places the Narrows is only 18 feet wide. In the middle of the desert, Zion is an oasis of rivers and streams. Hidden springs seep out through the cliffs at Weeping Rock and run like tears down the canyon wall. In the summertime, the cracks and ledges along these walls are alive with bright red, pink, and yellow wildflowers. One of the first Mormon pioneers to visit these canyons was so taken with the area he named it Zion—a safe place away from the troubles of the world

Z z

Z is for Zion,
where canyons run narrow and deep,
and wildflowers bloom
on desert walls that weep.

So there are our national parks,
in an alphabet from A to Z,
places of beauty and wonder
that belong to you and me.

David Domeniconi

David Domeniconi grew up in San Francisco and graduated from San Francisco State College. He is the author of *G is for Golden: A California Alphabet*, published in 2002. His illustrated travel column, "Travelog," is a regular feature in the *Santa Barbara News-Press*. He and his wife, Janet, live in the Alexander Valley near Healdsburg, California where they own and operate an art gallery, J. Howell Fine Art.

Pam Carroll

Born and raised in Southern California, Pamela Carroll embraces the traditional focus of realism and pictorial illusionism. Her style of painting has been greatly influenced by the early Dutch Masters and the American Realists from the Second School of Philadelphia. *M is for Majestic* is Pam's fifth children's book. She has also illustrated *A is for America: An American Alphabet*; *One Nation: America by the Numbers*; *S is for Star: A Christmas Alphabet*; and *G is for Golden: A California Alphabet*. She lives with her husband in Carmel, California, where she paints daily, and is an active member of the Carmel Art Association and Hauk Fine Arts in Pacific Grove, California.